DALE EARNHARDT
vs.
JEFF GORDON

KINGSTON, NEW YORK   NEW YORK, NEW YORK

Trading Paint

DALE EARNHARDT
vs.
JEFF GORDON

Classic Photos from a Classic Rivalry

GEORGE TIEDEMANN
TEXT BY MARK BECHTEL

To Sharon,
for her support and patience

SPORTS ILLUSTRATED® and *Total*/SPORTS ILLUSTRAT-
ED are registered trademarks of Time Inc.
Used under license.

For information about permission to reproduce sections
of this book, please write to:
Permissions
Total Sports Publishing
100 Enterprise Drive
Kingston, NY 12401
www.TotalSportsPublishing.com

COVER PHOTOGRAPH: George Tiedemann

TRADING PAINT
Editorial Director: Morin Bishop
   Project Editor: Jeff Labrecque
   Senior Editor: John Bolster
   Designers: Barbara Chilenskas, Vincent Mejia
   Copyreader: A. Lee Fjordbotten
   Reporters: Andrew Blaise, Kate Brash, Ward Calhoun
   Photography Editor: John Blackmar

TRADING PAINT was prepared by
Bishop Books, Inc.
611 Broadway
New York, New York 10012

ISBN 1-892129-99-X
Library of Congress Cataloging-in-Publication Data

Bechtel, Mark
   Trading paint: Dale Earnhardt vs. Jeff Gordon: classic photos from a classic rivalry /
Mark Bechtel; photos by George Tiedemann.
     p. cm.
    Includes index.
    ISBN 1-892129-99-X (pbk.)
     1. Earnhardt, Dale, 1951- 2. Gordon, Jeff, 1971- 3. Automobile racing drivers--United
States--Biography. 4. Automobile racing drivers--United States--Pictorial works. I.
Tiedemann, George. II. Title

  GV1032.A1 B35 2001
  769.72'092'273--dc21
  [B]   00-054432

Printed in Canada

Contents

Introduction

by Mark Bechtel

Despite a generation gap, conflicting tastes and styles, and drastically different backgrounds, Earnhardt and Gordon have developed a mutual respect for each other that belies the ruthlessness of Winston Cup racing. The sight of Earnhardt's black Chevy stalking Gordon's rainbow-colored car, as it did in the 1998 Pennsylvania 500 (above), is a major attraction for NASCAR fans across the country.

Dale Earnhardt and Jeff Gordon are, quite simply, two of the best drivers ever to sit behind the wheel of a stock car. Past that, they don't have a whole lot in common. You don't have to look any farther than at their cars to see just how different they really are. Earnhardt commands a jet-black Chevrolet, a dark cloud that circles the track and sends the fear of God into other drivers when it appears in their rearview mirrors. Gordon also pilots a Chevrolet, but the explosion of brilliant colors that marks his car gives him an unthreatening, sunny aura. And that, in a nutshell, is what makes their rivalry so interesting. Although they have had some fine head-to-head

matchups on the track, it is their disparate personalities and antithetical images that have fueled their rivalry. Most racing fans rabidly associate themselves with one or the other—almost never with both.

Earnhardt is old school, something of a throwback to the days when stock car drivers were bootleggers and outlaws—the kind of guys who would just as soon go through you as around you. His father, Ralph, always had a way with cars, under the hood as well as in the driver's seat. "As a boy I remember standing on the tailgate of a pickup truck down in Columbia, watching my daddy race against David Pearson, Lee Petty, all of 'em," Earnhardt

Handsome, articulate, clean-cut and savvy, Gordon attracted a new generation to NASCAR but alienated others who resented the ease with which he ascended to the top.

The sacrifices Bickford made for Jeff, and the steely manner in which he made them, left some with the impression that his stepson was spoiled, a store-bought champion. As a kid, Jeff had a stable of race cars and a seemingly unlimited travel budget, and the favorable circumstances under which he raced continued when he moved on to bigger and better things. His first—and so far only—Winston Cup ride was with Rick Hendrick, an owner known for not scrimping on expenses. His first crew chief, Ray Evernham, was a mechanical genius. His crew, the Rainbow Warriors, was composed of hired guns, athletes trained to come in on race day to get him in and out of the pits in a hurry. In the eyes of his detractors it all added up to a big strike against Gordon—that he was somehow manufactured to race.

Earnhardt, on the other hand, came up through the ranks under much more trying circumstances. He had a family to support at 17. Most lessons he learned by keeping his eyes and ears open. But

said many years ago. "I come from where they been."

Gordon, on the other hand, comes from California. But like Earnhardt, he got into racing because of his dad. "I always wanted to race, but I couldn't afford it," said Gordon's stepfather, John Bickford. "I was living my dreams through Jeff. His being small made it obvious he'd never be a football player. So I taught him the only thing I knew, how to race." Bickford even uprooted his family and moved them across the country to Indiana, because it was easier for his teenage stepson to race there. "Decisions weren't based on emotion," said Bickford. "I approached it from a professional standpoint. This wasn't about having fun. If we want to have fun, we'll go to Disney World."

for the most part, he says, his prowess wasn't acquired; it was just innate. "I haven't got but a 9th-grade education," he said. "If someone comes up alongside me when I'm at top speed, it suddenly changes the very airflow around me. It's a dramatic change. I can actually hear this mysterious force very clearly. Perhaps it's the wind. And I can feel them getting on or off the gas. And yet, somehow, I don't quite know how to explain it, somehow all this is natural to me. I was born to do this."

If NASCAR were a Western movie, Gordon would be in the white hat; Earnhardt's would, of course, be black. But the sport has always had an outlaw chic, which has made Earnhardt one of its most popular figures for two decades.

"Earnhardt is the resurrected Confederate soldier," said Charlotte Motor Speedway president Humpy Wheeler. "Where [Richard] Petty was always compliant, Earnhardt will stand his ground and say, 'I'm not going to do that.' And the people who love him are the people who are told, every day, what to do and what not to do, and they've got all those rules and regulations to go by. That just draws them closer to him."

Gordon, on the other hand, can thank his movie-star looks, as well as his superior driving skills, for his popularity. When Rick Hendrick first met Gordon he was floored. "I was almost in a daze," said Hendrick. "Jeff had it all. It was just scary. He's good looking, and I can't believe how well he handled himself at age 20. ... What I found was a mature young guy who was kind of humble—a little bashful. A sponsor's dream." Gordon's boyish good looks didn't go unnoticed. During his rookie season he won a 125-mile qualifying race at Daytona. In Victory Lane he and a Miss Winston model, Brooke Sealey, caught each other's eye. Relationships between drivers and Winston models are verboten, so the two canoodled in secret. They were engaged a year after they met, married following Gordon's second season.

The storybook romance just enhanced Gordon's squeaky-clean image. When he won his first race, at Charlotte in 1994, he wept in Victory Lane, which led a few veteran drivers—Earnhardt included—to make fun of him. When he won the Winston Cup in 1995 Earnhardt quipped, "Guess they'll serve milk at our banquet in New York this year." At the banquet, Gordon shed a few more tears, and a few more jokes were made. At the time, he was 24 years old, married to a gorgeous model

and at the top of his profession. Needless to say, some fans—especially those of Earnhardt—began jumping on the anti-Gordon bandwagon. Booing at tracks became common, and while you might not approve, you can at least understand it. The kid seemed to have everything, and he could do no wrong. He was too good.

Within the sport, however, the rough treatment rubbed many the wrong way. "I am, in a lot of ways, a Jeff Gordon fan," said driver Mark Martin. "I approve of him, the way he lives his life, the way he conducts himself and everything else. If the fans who don't like Jeff Gordon—if they think they don't like him, well, they should just imagine how a different personality could be in his situation. It hurts

Gordon's arrival to the Winston Cup circuit in the early '90s may have denied Earnhardt his treasured eighth title, but it also succeeded in accomplishing what many had thought impossible: It made cheering for Earnhardt— NASCAR's traditional bad guy— acceptable.

Since 1986 Earnhardt (left, celebrating his 1998 Daytona 500 victory) and Gordon (above, celebrating his 1997 Daytona win) have combined for nine of the last 15 Winston Cup championships.

me to hear him booed because he's good."

Love him or hate him, Gordon was great for the sport's Q rating. In 1998, he won four races in a row, tying the modern NASCAR record. When Gordon attempted to break it in August at Bristol, track officials estimated they could have sold 300,000 tickets if they had the room—much of the interest generated by rabid anti-Gordon fans. Nineteen years earlier, Earnhardt had won his first Winston Cup race at the same track before a crowd of only 26,000.

That's what the Earnhardt-Gordon rivalry

boils down to: fans of one driver cheering against the other almost as hard as they root on their guy. The two drivers have developed a healthy respect for each other; their fans, however, keep the rivalry going. There are certainly days when Gordon fans wish that Earnhardt would take his Intimidator act and ride off into the sunset, just like Earnhardt backers often rue the day Gordon and his merry band of Rainbow Warriors showed up on the scene. But make no mistake. Had the two not appeared on the scene together, NASCAR wouldn't have been the same.

Racing was the Earnhardt family passion if not the family business. Young Dale (left, standing in front of his father's race car) spent much of his youth working on cars and hanging around racetracks. Yet his path to the top was rarely easy. By age 25 (opposite) he had been married twice, had endured the early death of his father, and had not yet won a major race.

Earnhardt: Racing's Rebel

by Mark Bechtel

Dale Earnhardt's earliest memory is of watching his father race. Ralph Earnhardt drove cars. He lived cars. In a garage that he built behind his Kannapolis, N.C., house, Ralph became as good a mechanic as he was a driver—and he was a great driver, winning over 350 career races at tracks of all shapes and sizes. Humpy Wheeler, owner of the Charlotte Motor Speedway, called him "perhaps the finest dirt track driver who ever lived."

"Following in his footsteps is all I've ever wanted to do," Dale said. But watching his father go off to the track every day while he had to go to school became more and more difficult for Dale as he grew older, so in the ninth grade he dropped out. "It was the only thing I ever let my daddy down over," he said. "He wanted me to finish. It

was the only thing he ever pleaded with me to do. But I was so hardheaded. For about a year-and-a-half after that, we didn't have a close relationship."

The hardheaded kid was married by the time he was 17 and divorced at 19. That year he began racing, driving on many of the same dirt tracks as his dad. He and his father rarely went head-to-head, though, because Dale was usually driving a junker owned by one of his friends. To pay the bills he worked as a welder and a mechanic on the side, and if that didn't bring in enough money to keep his racing operation—and his family—afloat, he'd borrow money on Thursday and hope to win enough on Friday and Saturday to repay it. His family, he said, "probably should have been on welfare."

Earnhardt remarried at 20, but it was far from a blissful union. By 1975, when he was 24, he had three kids and all kinds of trouble supporting them. "Racing cost me my second marriage because of the things I took away from my family," he said. In his own words, he was "wild and crazy, young and dumb." A pal summed him up thus: "He was the kind of guy who would wake you up at 3 a.m. blasting a shotgun in your yard."

On September 26, 1973, as he was rebuilding a carburetor in the garage in his backyard, Ralph Earnhardt died of a heart attack. He was only 44. Ralph's death broke Dale's heart—the two had reconciled after their falling out, and Ralph had been helping Dale with his racing career. But ironically it was Ralph's death that allowed Dale's career to take off. Dale took over his dad's shop, quit driving clunkers and started attracting attention. "[Dad's death] left me in a situation where I had to make it on my own," said Dale. "I'd give up everything I got if he were still alive, but I don't think I'd be where I am if he hadn't died."

In the summer of '75 Ed Negre gave Earnhardt a seat for the World 600 in Charlotte. Earnhardt started 33rd and finished 22nd. But his big break came in 1978. An owner named Will Cronkite was planning on letting a young driver named Willy T. Ribbs drive his car in the World 600. Shortly before the race, Ribbs was arrested for driving the wrong way on a one-way street and resisting arrest. Cronkite stripped him of the ride, giving it to Earnhardt. Earnhardt drove four races for Cronkite, with two top 10 finishes, and caught the attention of a California businessman named Rod Osterlund. Osterlund put Earnhardt behind the wheel for the next-to-last race of the season, in Atlanta, and Earnhardt finished fourth. Finally, he had a full-time ride with Osterlund.

Earnhardt finished eighth at Daytona in 1979 and impressed Jake Elder, a veteran crew chief who had worked for the likes of David Pearson, Darrell Waltrip and Benny Parsons. Elder was working with Buddy Baker's crew at the time, but hoping for his

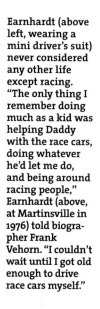

Earnhardt (above left, wearing a mini driver's suit) never considered any other life except racing. "The only thing I remember doing much as a kid was helping Daddy with the race cars, doing whatever he'd let me do, and being around racing people," Earnhardt (above, at Martinsville in 1976) told biographer Frank Vehorn. "I couldn't wait until I got old enough to drive race cars myself."

Dale Earnhardt

YEAR	STARTS	WINS	TOP 5	TOP 10	MONEY
1975	1	0	0	0	1,925
1976	2	0	0	0	3,085
1977	1	0	0	0	1,375
1978	5	0	1	2	20,145
1979	27	1	11	17	264,086
1980	31	5	19	24	588,926
1981	31	0	9	17	347,113
1982	30	1	7	12	375,325
1983	30	2	9	14	446,272
1984	30	2	12	22	616,788
1985	28	4	10	16	546,596
1986	29	5	16	23	1,783,880
1987	29	11	21	24	2,099,243
1988	29	3	13	19	1,214,089
1989	29	5	14	19	1,435,730
1990	29	9	18	23	3,083,056
1991	29	4	14	21	2,396,685
1992	29	1	6	15	915,463
1993	30	6	17	21	3,353,789
1994	31	4	20	25	3,300,733
1995	31	5	19	23	3,154,241
1996	31	2	13	17	2,285,926
1997	32	0	7	16	2,151,909
1998	33	1	5	13	2,588,400
1999	34	3	7	21	2,682,089
2000	34	2	13	24	2,605,645
Total	675	76	281	428	38,262,514

own car. After watching Earnhardt race, Elder quit Baker's crew and came aboard. With Elder as crew chief, Earnhardt learned quickly. There were some growing pains: At Pocono in July 1979 he was leading the Coca-Cola 500 when a tire blew, sending him into the wall. He broke both collarbones, suffered a concussion and received severe bruises on his neck and chest that forced him to miss four races. But he also picked up his first career win, at Bristol, in just his 16th career start. Elder called it the biggest win of his own long career.

Earnhardt, who went on to become the Grand National Rookie of the Year, couldn't help but think about his father, the man most responsible for getting him on the long road that led to Bristol's Victory Lane. "I know somewhere there's a fellow that's got a big smile," he said, "and is mighty, mighty proud and even more happy than I am, if that's possible."

Earnhardt, driving number 2, didn't win the Firecracker 400 in 1980 (below), but he did win five races that year to claim his first championship.

If Earnhardt didn't experience immediate success, his patience was duly rewarded when he became the first driver to win the Rookie of the Year title and the points title in successive years.

Earnhardt's outstanding rookie season made Osterlund eager to quash any thoughts another owner might have about swooping in and taking his driver. He signed Earnhardt to a five-year contract before the start of the 1980 season, giving what looked to the 28-year-old to be a stable home for the foreseeable future. And it was, for a while. Earnhardt won a couple of races in March, putting himself in the thick of the points race. But then one May morning, Elder walked into the shop and announced he was quitting. Finding a new crew chief on short notice was not easy. The job went to Doug Richert, who had been with the Osterlund operation for four years—ever since he was 16. One of Elder's complaints before he left was that his crew was too green. Now it was going to be run by a 20-year-old.

Green or not, Earnhardt and Richert knew what they were doing. What the team lacked in experience Earnhardt made up for in guts. "Dale Earnhardt makes that car run," said David Ifft, crew chief for Benny Parsons. "He's been driving like a wild man to make up for a lack of horse-power all year. Been going into the corners deeper and just throwing it the rest of the way around. Thing is, he's good enough to get away with it."

The new team didn't burst out of the gate, but they were consistent, and heading into the final race of the season in Ontario, Calif., they found themselves leading the season points race. In Ontario, though, the team made two uncharacteristic mistakes in the pits, which put Earnhardt outside of the top 10 and in danger of losing the crown to the red-hot Cale Yarborough, who was running up front. But Earnhardt battled back to finish fifth in the race and won the season title. Not only was Earnhardt the first man to win the Rookie of the Year award and the Winston Cup championship in successive seasons, but his crew won the Sears Craftsman pit championship by turning in the fastest stops in 10 selected races during the season.

"We had something to prove," said Richert. "We were supposed to fall on our butts, go down the tubes. We didn't. There was a lot of adrenaline flowing. We knew we could do the job."

Earnhardt not only proved himself a champion in 1980, but he also established himself as someone who couldn't be pushed around. At Martinsville in late September, he and Dave Marcis, whom he had replaced on Osterlund's team, tangled near the midpoint of the race. Earnhardt refused to back down from the veteran, banging back every time he took a hit. Eventually he spun completely around, but he kept his car up to speed and went on to win the race. "I came here to race, not to stroke for points," he said. Others took notice. "He has more damn nerve than a sore tooth," said veteran Buddy Baker. It was just a small taste of things to come.

The successes of 1980 made the following year that much more torturous for Earnhardt. Midway through the season Osterlund sold the team to Jim Stacy, who

At the Southern 500 in 1985 (above) Earnhardt slammed into the wall and failed to finish, but it was his take-no-prisoners, all-or-nothing style that earned him the respect of fellow drivers like the late Neil Bonnett (opposite, left).

made significant changes. After only four races Earnhardt wanted out. Richard Childress, who had been driving his own car, offered to give up the seat for Earnhardt and serve strictly as owner. Earnhardt accepted, but the change did not yield a return to Victory Lane. He could do no better than fourth over the last 15 races, and finished seventh in the championship race. "I don't care who it is," he said. "When you've been accustomed to winning, winning big, and suddenly you're not anymore, it's going to make you feel down. That's human nature."

Earnhardt went on to drive for Bud Moore the following year, but he failed to recapture the magic of 1980's title-winning season. He finished 12th and eighth in two years with Moore before going back to Childress full time.

The dominant driver at the time was Darrell Waltrip, who had won 40 races and three titles from 1981 through '85, compared to nine and zero for Earnhardt. Waltrip had taken a few verbal potshots at Earnhardt for his rough driving—"You ought to get 10 bonus points for taking Earnhardt out of a race"—but the two had avoided any major entanglements on the track. That all changed in Richmond on Feb. 23, 1986. In the Miller 400, Waltrip tried to pass for the lead and Earnhardt smacked the right rear of Waltrip's car as he drove by. Both drivers were knocked out of the race, and Waltrip and his owner, Junior Johnson, were livid. "You can't race with a fool like that!" Johnson roared. "It was no different than if he had put a loaded gun to Darrell's head and pulled the trigger." The incident

In the final 10-lap segment of the Winston, Earnhardt knocked Bill Elliott into the wall. Elliott blew a tire a few laps later, allowing Earnhardt to waltz to the win. On the cooldown lap, though, Elliott heated up. He drove back onto the track, plowed into Earnhardt and tried to block him from reaching Victory Lane. "You race hard and you do everything you can, you even rub and bang with people, but you don't try to kill them," said Geoff Bodine, who crashed when Earnhardt bumped Elliott into him. "If [Earnhardt] thinks that's racing, he's sick."

Although Elliott's actions at Charlotte were indefensible, Earnhardt, who cruised to the title in '87, wasn't winning any friends on the track—not that he cared. The following year, he and Bodine tangled again at Charlotte, and when Bodine ended up in the wall, NASCAR put Earnhardt in a "penalty box" for five laps. Message received. Earnhardt did most of his intimidating by reputation from that point on.

After a two-year stretch in which he finished third and second, Earnhardt again won back-to-back season titles in 1990 and '91, giving him five championships. Only the King, Richard Petty, who had won seven, had more. But for all his victories, Earnhardt never could win the sport's biggest race, the Daytona 500. He had come close—a cut tire a mile from the finish in '90 allowed Derrike Cope to win—but never could find a way to take the checkered flag. It looked like a good bet that Earnhardt would break that streak in '92 and win a third straight title as well. But he accomplished neither. Earnhardt finished a disappointing ninth in the 500, and it was more of the same throughout the season. He won only once and finished 12th in the points standings, his worst showing in 10 years.

Following the season his crew chief, Kirk Shelmerdine, who had been with Earnhardt and Childress from the beginning, abruptly retired. That sparked rumors that maybe

forever altered the Earnhardt-Waltrip rivalry. Earnhardt went on to win five races, $1.7 million, and his second championship in '86. He also picked up a new nickname—the Intimidator.

The next year he singlehandedly turned the Winston—NASCAR's version of the All-Star Game—into one of the most action-packed races the sport has ever seen. He had already won six races that season—the best start in NASCAR history—when he arrived in Charlotte on May 17, and he had done so in typically brash fashion. Coo Coo Marlin, an old-school driver whose son, Sterling, had been knocked out by Earnhardt earlier that year in a race at Bristol, said he wished it were the good ol' days, when Earnhardt would have been taken "out behind some barn" and dealt with appropriately. Neil Bonnett said, "If I ever catch him, I'm gonna knock the s--- out of him." And Bonnett was one of Earnhardt's best friends.

Earnhardt (above, at Watkins Glen in 1988) prided himself on his reputation as a tough, uncompromising Man in Black. After his third-place finish at Atlanta in 1990 (left), he became only the second man to win four championships.

Childress and Earnhardt would split as well. Instead, they decided to rededicate themselves. Andy Petree, who had been Harry Gant's crew chief, was hired to replace Shelmerdine. "Childress went to every man in the shop and had about a two-hour discussion with each of them," Earnhardt said. "He asked them what they thought about the shop and our situation since Kirk announced that he was going to quit. He asked them how they'd improve the situa-tion. Whether it was the engine man or the janitor, he wanted to know what changes would make us better. That's what makes Richard Childress a good car owner."

But as they headed into the 1993 season, it was unclear whether the team's dedication would be enough to bring about a return to prominence. Bouncing back from adversity is never easy—and there was a new driver coming on the scene who was going to make it even more difficult.

Gordon steered his Silver Crown dirt car (opposite) through Turn 2 of the Phoenix International Roadway on his way to winning the Copper World Classic in February 1991. He took an evening off from racing to attend the 1989 Tri-West High School prom in Pittsboro, Indiana. Gordon and Deena Waters (left) were named the king and queen of the prom.

Gordon: The Natural

by Mark Bechtel

When he sat behind the wheel of a stock car for the first time in his life, at a driving school in Rockingham, N.C., run by former NASCAR driver Buck Baker, 18-year-old Jeff Gordon was smitten. He had always loved cars, but this one was special. "The car was different from anything I was used to," Gordon said. "It was so big and heavy. It felt very fast but very smooth. I loved it." That day changed Gordon's life.

Since the age of five Gordon had been groomed to race cars. He was a prodigious talent, but he dreamed of racing open-wheel at Indianapolis. He had never given much thought to racing full-bodied stock cars. At Baker's school he realized that he not only liked it but was also good at it. An owner named Hugh Connerly was so impressed with Gordon's proficiency

behind the wheel that he offered him a ride in his Pontiac in the 1990 AC Delco 200 Busch Series event in Rockingham. That race set in motion a chain of events that propelled him to stock car greatness.

Gordon had been a racer as long as he could remember. He had started out on a BMX bike, but when he was four, his mom, Carol, took that away from him. "At BMX events they were hauling kids away in ambulances all the time," she said.

To make up for the loss, Gordon's stepfather, John Bickford, went out and bought him a race car, a six-foot quarter-midget. Since the cars were demonstrably safer, mom was okay with the idea. Within three years Bickford and Gordon had a stable of eight cars and were racing 52 weeks a year. "We were the Roger Penske of quarter-

midgets," said Bickford. They won the national championship in 1979, and two years later Jeff moved up to go-karts. He beat 16- and 17-year-olds so regularly that other parents, half in jest, suggested that the nine-year-old was really a short 20-year-old. After being routinely humiliated, drivers simply quit racing against Gordon. He went back to quarter-midgets and won the championship again when he was 10, but a pre-adolescent malaise was setting in. "You get to be 12 years old and you realize you've been in quarter-midgets for eight years," said Gordon. "What's next? I was getting older, not knowing what I wanted to do next."

The answer was to build a $25,000 sprint car, a beast of a machine that could run at a few tracks in the Midwest that didn't have age requirements because, as Gordon said, "nobody was fool enough to drive that young." By 1986, when Jeff was 14, the family had a decision to make. They lived in Vallejo, in Northern California, and committing to races in the Midwest was logistically just too grueling. So the family packed up and moved to Pittsboro, a small town of 1,000 or so in Indiana corn country, a mere 15 miles from the Indianapolis Motor Speedway.

In 1989, Gordon won the first midget event he entered, beating a handful of Indy 500 drivers in the Night Before the 500, at Indianapolis Raceway Park. The next year, at age 19, he won the USAC full midget championship and took the Night Before the 500 again.

Several of his wins came on ESPN's *Thursday Night Thunder* broadcasts. It was the beginning of the phenomenon of race car drivers becoming personalities. "Television promotion is so important in any sport, but especially to young guys in racing," said Gordon in 1991. "I don't know what would've happened without it [ESPN]. Last year was just an unbelievable year, and a lot of my wins happened to be

on television. We used each other, though. I used ESPN to promote my career; they used me to promote *Thursday Night*. But it's like anything else; you've gotta use your assets." In the years to come, using his assets would be something Gordon did better than anyone.

Gordon was still thinking about racing Indy cars at that point, but in the summer of 1990 his parents suggested he give NASCAR a thought. On a whim, he went to Baker's school and immediately decided that stock cars were for him. He took Connerly up on his offer to run at Rockingham, and he put the car on the

Gordon, driving a white Baby Ruth–sponsored car, won 11 poles and three races in 1992 to finish fourth in the Busch Series points standings.

Jeff Gordon

YEAR	STARTS	WINS	TOP 5	TOP 10	MONEY
1992	1	0	0	0	6,285
1993	30	0	7	11	765,168
1994	31	2	7	14	1,779,523
1995	31	7	10	16	4,347,343
1996	31	10	21	24	3,428,485
1997	32	10	22	23	6,375,658
1998	33	13	26	28	5,158,392
1999	34	7	18	21	5,121,361
2000	34	3	11	22	2,588,455
Total	257	52	122	159	29,570,670

outside of Row 1. "I'm so damn happy right now I'm about to cry," Gordon said after qualifying. "I'm just having a hard time right now believing that this is happening to me. I never dreamed I could do anything like this."

Gordon didn't finish the race, but the folks at Ford were impressed enough to offer him a full Busch Series ride in 1991. Indy cars were suddenly on the back burner. "A lot of thought went into my decision," Gordon said at the time. "Right now, Indy cars, they're great to race, and it takes real talent to run up front, but there just aren't many opportunities to get involved."

For the '91 Busch season, Ford put Gordon in a car owned by Bill Davis. One

of the crew members Davis recruited was a Jersey Shore gearhead named Ray Evernham. Evernham dreamed of being a driver and had done a fair amount of racing at tracks in New Jersey. However, a serious wreck in 1991 left him with a brain-stem injury, ending his career as a driver. But when Evernham hadn't been behind the wheel of a car, he had been under the hood of one. He had experience in the IROC series as a mechanic and had picked up a host of chassis-setup secrets from hanging around tracks for most of his adult life. He and Gordon clicked immediately. "What impressed me most about Ray right from the start was that he had driven race cars," said Gordon. "He knew the cars

No one paid much attention to Evernham and Gordon as they prepared for their first Winston Cup race, the 1992 Hooters 500 in Atlanta. As fate would have it, Richard Petty, winner of seven championships and 200 races, was driving in the final race of his historic career that day.

Gordon had excelled at every level by the time he reached Atlanta in November 1992 (left). But his 31st-place finish in the Hooters 500 demonstrated how far he still had to go.

mechanically better than I did, but he could still relate to me."

Their first collaboration, however, was brief: Evernham soon joined Alan Kulwicki's crew, Ford's top team at the time, as a chassis specialist, while Gordon went on to win the Busch Rookie of the Year award in 1991 without him. The following February, Evernham quit after getting into a shouting match with Kulwicki at Daytona. At Gordon's insistence, Ford engineers tracked Evernham down and persuaded him to stay on the team as Gordon's mentor.

With Evernham on board, Gordon began to excel—he won three Busch races in 1992—and racing people took notice. At the Busch race in Atlanta in March of 1992, Gordon was constantly careening through the corners, running way too loose but still hanging on. He caught the eye of several onlookers, including a few car owners. Rick Hendrick, for one, was impressed. He told the people with him, "You just can't drive a car that loose." But Gordon did and he won the race.

Winston Cup job offers soon started coming in. Car owner Jack Roush called Bickford, who rebuffed him for a very significant reason. Bickford told the owner that his stepson and Evernham were a package deal. Roush replied that drivers didn't pick their crew chiefs, especially not 20-year-old drivers. Bickford simply hung up. Roush called back to try to smooth things over, but there was no deal. Hendrick was much more accommodating. When he agreed to bring Evernham along in May of '92, Gordon signed.

Saying no to Roush in favor of Hendrick meant switching from Ford to Chevy. "Ford gave me a lot in terms of support and backing," said Gordon. "But they didn't make me the racer I am. I trust completely that Rick's the guy who's going to help me become the best I can."

The move ruffled a few feathers. Michael Kranefuss, then Ford's director of special-vehicle operations and later a car owner, said, "Why would a young kid, who has won over 600 races, be so blinded and team with somebody who couldn't make a two-car team work and now wants to make a three-car team?"

As he prepared to embark on his Winston Cup career, Gordon had a ride on a team with deep pockets but little proven success. He had his crew chief of choice, he had an impressive curriculum vitae and he had people out to get him. It was the beginning of a legendary career, but it was also the end of Gordon's innocence.

New Kid on the Block

1993–1995

Gordon (opposite), hiding his youth behind a moustache, celebrated with Linda Vaughn and his mother (opposite, left and right, respectively) in '93 after he became the youngest driver to win a Daytona 125-mile qualifying race. Earnhardt (left) would win his sixth Winston Cup title that year, but Gordon's emergence threatened his run of dominance.

New Kid on the Block

by Mark Bechtel

Jeff Gordon's Winston Cup debut, on November 15, 1992, was significant in retrospect, but at the time, the 21-year-old prodigy was merely a sideshow. After 1,185 starts, 200 victories and seven championships, Richard Petty was ending his historic career. The Winston Cup points race in 1992, therefore, had developed into a struggle for who would succeed Petty as the sport's dominant figure. A couple of veterans, Bill Elliott and Harry Gant, were still in contention, but more recent arrivals Alan Kulwicki and Davey Allison were locked in a tight duel for the title. Petty finished 35th that day in Atlanta, and Kulwicki held off Allison and Elliott to win the championship. Gordon placed a forgettable 31st, but he nevertheless impressed the sport's departing immortal. "Watch out

for the Gordon kid," Petty said. "He's the future."

The torch was being passed, and the sport's future never looked better. But the following April, Kulwicki would be killed when his private plane crashed in Tennessee. Barely three months later, Allison would be gone, too, the victim of a helicopter crash in Talladega. Gordon, who had expected to be one of a handful of young drivers leading the sport into the next century, had lost two of his most talented competitors.

When Gordon made his first Daytona 500 appearance in 1993, driver Sterling Marlin proclaimed him to be "more fortunate than any rookie to come this way in a long time." Rick Hendrick, who had lured Gordon from the Ford stable in '92, was known for his

Gordon's victory in the inaugural '94 Brickyard 400 (left) before a crowd of more than 300,000 was another sign that NASCAR had arrived as a major sports attraction.

deep pockets and for turning out good motors. "A good engine is going to make you look good, particularly at Daytona," said Marlin. With a Hendrick engine under his car's hood, Gordon became the youngest winner in a Daytona qualifying race. In the second race Earnhardt, who was looking to bounce back from a disastrous '92 season, started his Speed Week off in typical fashion, winning his qualifier for the fourth straight year.

So on Sunday, the young kid and the old master started alongside each other on the second row, and they spent most of the afternoon in fairly close quarters. With two laps left Earnhardt led, but Gordon was attached to his rear like a bumper sticker. On the 198th lap Dale Jarrett passed Gordon for second place and was prepared to make a run at Earnhardt. Gordon had a decision to make. He could go with Jarrett and try to push past Earnhardt, or he could

stay with the Intimidator and try to push him past Jarrett. He stayed where he was, and it turned out to be a mistake. Geoff Bodine sidled up behind Jarrett, and their two-car train inched past Earnhardt and Gordon. When the checkered flag fell, Jarrett led, Earnhardt was second and Gordon had been shuffled back to fifth. "I was going to go for Earnhardt with two laps left, but when Jarrett went early it messed up my plans," Gordon said. "When he pulled even with the number 3 car, I had to make a decision. Nine out of 10 times, the right one would be to go with Dale. I guess this was the other time, because it didn't work out, but it was one heck of a day."

Still, the race sent a clear signal that Gordon had arrived. It also left little doubt that Earnhardt had returned. In the Winston Cup points race, Earnhardt established a huge lead over Rusty Wallace, who had been hampered by several terrible finishes. Then, with his sixth points title all but wrapped up, Earnhardt had a couple of disasters of his own. His 304-point lead with eight races left shrank to 82 points after he finished 27th and 29th in consecutive outings. But Earnhardt recovered to finish in the top four in each of the next four races, giving him his sixth Winston Cup championship—one shy of Richard Petty's record.

The following year, Gordon made a few strides toward becoming a factor in the championship race. He won his first race, the Coca-Cola 600, in Charlotte in May. Then, in August, he won the inaugural Brickyard 400 at the Indianapolis Motor Speedway. He wrapped up that race when brothers Brett and Geoff Bodine, who were in the midst of an off-the-track feud, tangled. "I saw [Geoff] have his misfortune and I thought, Well, all I got to do is be nice and smooth and ride it out from here," Gordon said.

Although Gordon denied Earnhardt a record-breaking eighth championship in 1995, the Intimidator was not ready to concede the crown just yet.

Being nice and smooth was not Gordon's forte during his first two years. He had 21 DNFs, mostly from wrecks. "He doesn't use the car up," said his crew chief Ray Evernham. "He knows how to save it. But sometimes he puts the car in a position he shouldn't be in."

In 1995 Gordon took better care of his car. He won three of the first six races of the season, and fans became excited at the prospect of a shootout between Gordon and Earnhardt, who had won his seventh Winston Cup title in '94. The two finished one–two in two races in '95, but neither was a door-to-door affair. The first came in the season's seventh race, at North Wilkesboro, which Earnhardt won by 13.48 seconds over Gordon. "It's amazing to beat Boy Wonder," he said.

Earnhardt's sarcasm was understandable.

It wasn't that he was jealous of the attention Gordon was getting; Earnhardt had his own ardent following. The problem was, this kid was standing between him and an unprecedented eighth Winston Cup championship.

Gordon's fast start gave him a comfortable cushion in the points race, and midway through the season Evernham faced questions about the possibility of unseating Earnhardt. "We're still too young to think about it," said Evernham. "But we might not be too young to do it."

By the time Gordon and Earnhardt got to Atlanta for the season-ending NAPA 500, Gordon's lead was 147 points. Earnhardt's only chance was to win that race, lead the most laps and hope Gordon fell on his face. All Gordon had to do was finish better than 41st or lead a single lap

NEW KID ON THE BLOCK

to wrap up the title. Earnhardt did what he had to do, winning the race and leading a whopping 268 of 328 laps. But Gordon led on Lap 61, when he stayed out an extra lap during green-flag pit stops and earned the five-point bonus for leading a lap. When Sterling Marlin pitted, Gordon officially took the lead, and Evernham shouted over the radio, "That's it! That's it! That's the championship. Pit! Pit! Pit!"

After the race, Gordon had nothing but praise for his rival's performance. "Earnhardt is incredible," Gordon said. "The way that guy drove the last five or 10 races, he was very aggressive and he did what he needed to do. But we put together a total package, a total season, and it was impossible to bring us down."

Earnhardt was slightly less effusive in his praise of the 24-year-old champ, refusing to lump Gordon in with the greats just yet and pointing out that the points race wasn't even that dramatic. "Darrell Waltrip and I had some great championships, and I had some great ones with Rusty [Wallace]," Earnhardt said. "The one I had the most fun with was racing Mark Martin [in 1990 when Earnhardt won his fourth title by 26 points]. We raced competitive, side-by-side throughout the last part of the season. This one is one we lost because we had problems, not because we raced and lost. We never really went fender-to-fender with him and raced down to the wire."

There would be plenty of time for fender-to-fender racing, though. The 44-year-old Intimidator wasn't about to let up in his quest for that eighth championship. But the kid would prove to be awfully hard to rattle.

Remembering Earnhardt's jab at his youth and wholesome image, Gordon made a point to toast the seven-time champ with a glass of milk at the NASCAR awards banquet.

Wonder Boy

Dale Jarrett may have won, but 21-year-old Jeff Gordon was the center of attention at the 1993 Daytona 500

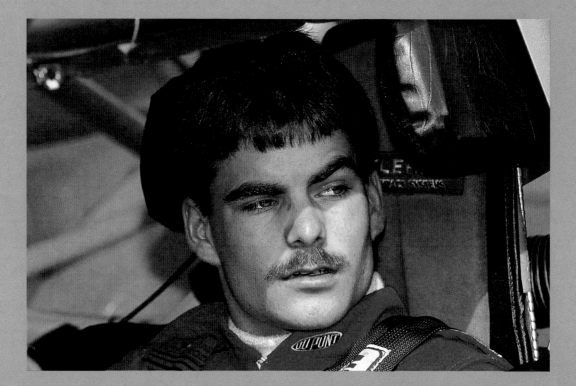

2.14.93—During the final laps of the Daytona 500, Jeff Gordon gambled that Dale Earnhardt would show him the way to Victory Lane. But the decision backfired as Dale Jarrett beat them both to the checkered flag. Earnhardt held on for second place—another near-miss at Daytona—and Gordon, who won one of the Daytona qualifying races, dropped to fifth place.

Despite his bad luck at the end, Gordon was thrilled with his performance. "Winning the

[qualifying race] was one thing," Gordon said. "But to come back and finish fifth in the Daytona 500, it's just amazing."

Earnhardt was left to ponder another Daytona heartbreaker. He led entering the final lap, but he allowed Jarrett to slip by on the inside near Turn 1 and lost by .19 of a second. "Everybody wanted to know if I could finally win the Daytona 500 on my 15th try," Earnhardt said. "I guess it'll take at least 16 now."

The Kid and the Intimidator

Gordon (24) and Earnhardt (3) battled all day but teamed up in the final stages of the 500. "He loves to run with Earnhardt," said Gordon's car's owner, Rick Hendrick. "He looks for him and tries to run with him."

Going for Brooke

The future Mrs. Gordon, Miss Winston model Brooke Sealey (left), helped reward Gordon after he became the youngest driver to win a Daytona 500 qualifier.

"I've never seen anyone this good at this age in all the years I was a driver. His talent, and his feel for a race car, he will be good wherever he goes. He is going to do great."

—*Dale Earnhardt*

Almost Famous

Prior to his first Daytona start, Gordon—sporting a moustache and an Intimidator-esque pair of shades—and crew chief Ray Evernham were asking, "Can it get any better than this?" The answer: Yes.

Staking His Claim

Dale Earnhardt's 10th-place finish at the Hooters 500 clinched his sixth season title—one shy of Richard Petty's record

11.14.93—The race was scheduled for 500 miles, but the drama was over well before that. When T.W. Taylor officially dropped out on Lap 155 of the Hooters 500, Dale Earnhardt won his sixth Winston Cup championship and a $1.25 million bonus. Earnhardt entered the season's final race leading Rusty Wallace by 126 points and needed to finish in the top 34 to clinch the championship. After Taylor's elimination guaranteed that, Earnhardt's team flashed a banner congratulating him. "They didn't tell me anything, but they had that banner up over the pits, so I knew," Earnhardt said.

Earnhardt ran into trouble in Lap 225 as he tried to catch the leaders—banging with Greg Sacks on the third turn—and settled for 10th. Not everyone was so lucky. Jeff Gordon was one of 15 drivers who failed to finish as there were a record-tying 11 caution flags.

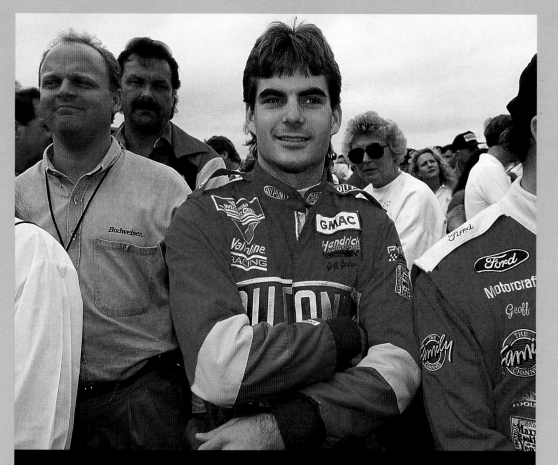

Slippin' and Slidin'

Gordon, who crashed in practice and during the race, wasn't smiling when he discussed the slick surface of Atlanta's recently conditioned track. "You don't see good cars crash like you have this weekend. I'm just disgusted right now."

1993 Final Winston Cup Standings

	DRIVER	POINTS	EARNINGS ($)
1.	Dale Earnhardt (6)	4,526	3,353,789
2.	Rusty Wallace (10)	4,446	1,702,154
3.	Mark Martin (5)	4,150	1,657,662
4.	Dale Jarrett (1)	4,000	1,242,394
5.	Kyle Petty (1)	3,860	914,652
14.	Jeff Gordon (0)	3,447	765,168

Note: Victories in parentheses.

One Closer to the King

"Every single championship is precious to me,"
Earnhardt said. "But this one means a whole lot.
We came off a kind of bad year last year and
had a great year this year."

Homecoming

The largest crowd to attend a NASCAR event, 315,000, turned out at the Indianapolis Motor Speedway to watch fellow Hoosier Gordon win the richest payday in the sport's history: $613,000.

44

Coming-Out Party

Jeff Gordon, who grew up 15 miles from Indy and dreamed of racing there, made history by winning the inaugural Brickyard 400

8.6.94—One Indy Car driver compared racing stock cars at Indianapolis, the mecca of American open-wheel racing, to "running dogs at Churchill Downs." Despite this assessment more than 300,000 fans showed up for the inaugural Brickyard 400, as NASCAR entered a new era of high-profile racing.

Appropriately, 23-year-old Jeff Gordon, who grew up in Pittsboro—only 15 miles west of the track—won the race, battling Ernie Irvan until Irvan blew a tire on Lap 156. "All my life I've wanted to race here," Gordon said. "I prayed for that day. But when I decided to race stock cars instead of Indy cars, I thought my dream never would be fulfilled."

Dale Earnhardt, who started second, brushed the wall on the second lap and had to play catchup for most of the day. His efforts paid off: He finished fifth and moved into first place in the Winston Cup standings.

Victory Laps

Gordon treated the crowd to not one but two victory laps after he edged Brett Bodine at the finish. "I had to take an extra lap because I still couldn't control my emotions," Gordon said.

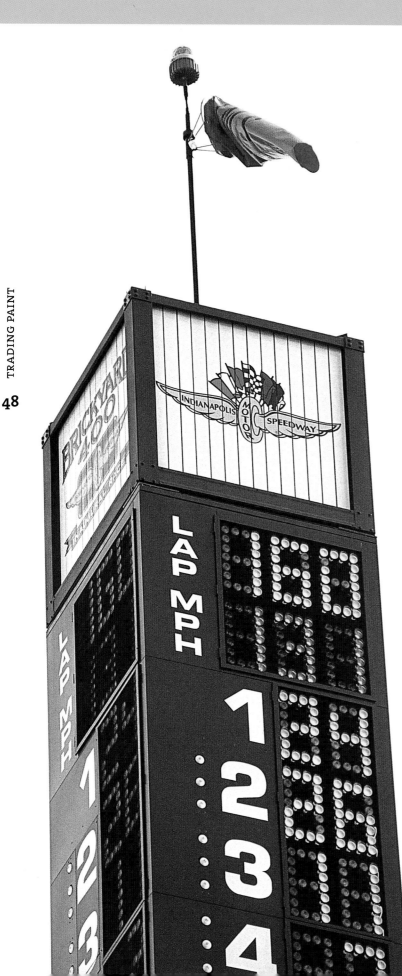

Gordon's heroics guaranteed that the first Brickyard 400 would not be the last. The scoring pylon at Indy (left), with Gordon's 24 on top, told the story at the end of the day.

"It is the top because I learned more growing up about the Indy 500 than the Daytona 500. This race is bigger than life as far as I'm concerned."

—*Jeff Gordon*

Seventh Heaven

Dale Earnhardt, who had already clinched his seventh championship, went all out during the season-ending Hooters 500.

11.13.94—Although Richard Petty will be known forever as the King, Dale Earnhardt made his own claim to racing royalty by winning his record-tying seventh Winston Cup crown. Earnhardt had clinched the title three weeks earlier at Rockingham with his fourth victory of the season. The Hooters 500, in Atlanta, was simply a coronation for the Intimidator. But that didn't prevent Earnhardt from going all out. "Every race we enter, we plan on winning,"

Earnhardt said. And he almost did. Although he started 30th, Earnhardt moved up to finish second behind Mark Martin.

Earnhardt, who had won six of the last nine titles, seemed earnestly humbled to join Petty as the only seven-time champions. "I'm proud and honored to be in the same group with him," he said. "But he got us here and will always be The King. Nothing will ever take that away from him."

King of the Road

Earnhardt could afford to joke around with Jeff Gordon and Ray Evernham (opposite) prior to the Hooters 500; the title was already his. Number 3 had 20 top 5 finishes in 1994.

"I've driven against Richard Petty and I've driven against Dale Earnhardt, and let me tell you that Dale is far and away the best purebred stock car driver I ever saw. He can do more with a race car than anyone I ever raced against."

—Darrell Waltrip

Team Intimidator

"You can't say enough about [team owner] Richard Childress and this whole crew," Earnhardt said. "They have given me the cars and support to win races and championships. All I do is drive 'em."

Racing Royalty

"When I talk about champions of NASCAR, then I want to have somebody who's a winner, and Earnhardt is definitely a winner," Petty (right) said. "He's got one speed and that's wide open, and that's the way a champion ought to be."

54

Dale on Dale

"In my opinion, Dale is the best pure racer I've ever seen," Dale Jarrett said. "He's the only driver I've ever watched who I feel was actually born a race car driver."

The Man in Black (Tie)

Earnhardt and his wife, Teresa, were the stars of the NASCAR Annual Banquet in New York. "Dale will go out of his way to help people, and I know he's really helped me out," Ernie Irvan said. "He's really a nice guy—he just doesn't want people to think that."

1994 Final Winston Cup Standings

	DRIVER	POINTS	EARNINGS ($)
1.	Dale Earnhardt (4)	4,694	3,400,733
2.	Mark Martin (2)	4,250	1,678,906
3.	Rusty Wallace (8)	4,207	1,959,072
4.	Kenny Schrader (0)	4,060	1,211,062
5.	Ricky Rudd (1)	4,050	1,044,441
8.	Jeff Gordon (0)	3,776	1,799,523

Note: Victories in parentheses.

Bristol Breakthrough

Jeff Gordon, written off as a superspeedway specialist, recorded his first career short-track victory at the Food City 500

4.2.95—"Our only goal today was to come out with the car in one piece," Jeff Gordon said. "We did that and a whole lot more."

Indeed, Gordon hadn't just performed poorly at Bristol, he'd never even finished a race there. At the Food City 500, however, he ran away with one, his third victory of the season. He led for 205 of the 500 laps, including the final 99, and finished nearly half a lap ahead of second-place Rusty Wallace. The convincing win

continued a run of dominance for Gordon: Of the 2,213 laps run thus far in 1995 Gordon led 1,002 of them.

Dale Earnhardt, who came to Bristol with a 67-point lead in the standings, hit the wall on Lap 116 while in second place and never threatened again. He got his car back on the track and finished 25th to retain a narrow 17-point lead in the standings. It was the first time in 1995 he didn't place in the top 5.

TRADING

One of Those Days

Earnhardt (3) battled all afternoon, even after an accident with Jeff Burton stripped his car of its front hood. He returned after extensive retooling to gather enough points to stay in first place for the season.

Denied

Dale Earnhardt shredded the field at the NAPA 500, but Jeff Gordon still became the youngest Winston Cup champion since 1950.

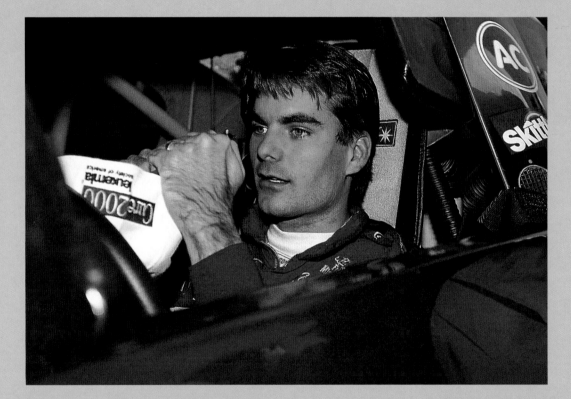

11.12.95—There had been whispers of a rivalry growing between Dale Earnhardt and Jeff Gordon ever since the clean-cut Californian joined the Winson Cup Series in 1992. Consider it official. Needing only to place in the top 41 or lead for one lap, Gordon finished 32nd and clinched his first championship. He also prevented Earnhardt from breaking Richard Petty's record of seven career titles.

But Earnhardt refused to concede the crown to his young rival without a fight. The Intimidator sent a message by offering the Boy Wonder a politically incorrect version of the No. 1 finger before the race and lapping him 14 times during it.

"I knew he had the thing won and that we weren't going to get our eighth championship this time," Earnhardt said. "It made me mad. I wanted to get this season over and get started with next year."

Easy Driver

"I knew I could pass him 50 times and it wouldn't make any difference," Earnhardt (bottom) said of Gordon (top). "He knew he had the championship locked up."

TEAM #24
CHECKLIST

☑ From Nobody To Upstart
☑ From Upstart To Contender
☑ From Contender To Winner
☐ From Winner To Champion
☐ From Champion To Dynasty

"To be able to finish ahead of that guy—Dale doesn't finish second very often—makes this championship more worthwhile."

—Jeff Gordon

1995 Final Winston Cup Standings

	DRIVER	POINTS	EARNINGS ($)
1.	Jeff Gordon (7)	4,614	4,347,343
2.	Dale Earnhardt (5)	4,580	3,154,241
3.	Sterling Marlin (3)	4,361	2,253,502
4.	Mark Martin (4)	4,320	1,893,519
5.	Rusty Wallace (2)	4,240	1,642,837

Note: Victories in parentheses.

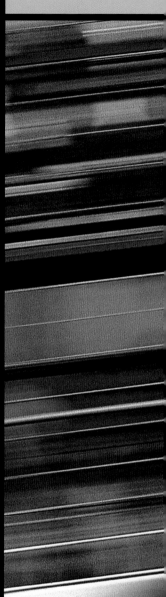

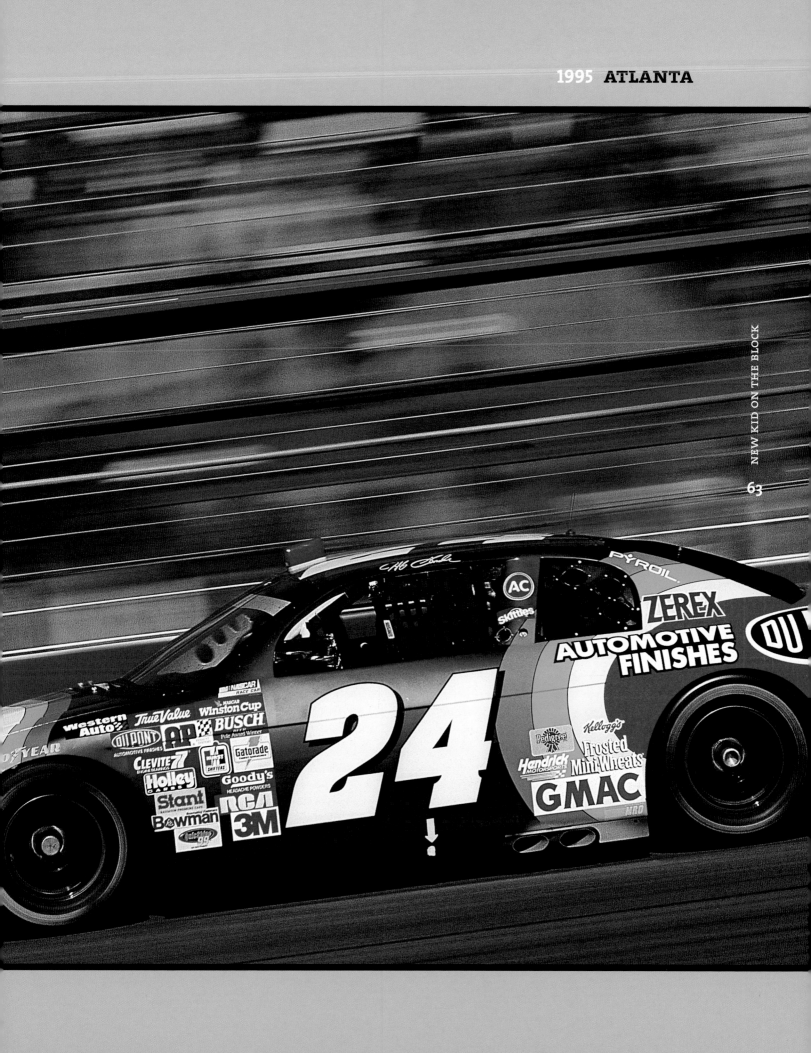

Changing of the Guard

1996–1998

Gordon and Earnhardt were both looking over their shoulders before the 1997 Pennsylvania 500 (opposite), but it was Gordon (left, peeking into Earnhardt's car prior to the 1996 Winston Select 500) who emerged as the sport's new superstar.

Changing of the Guard

by Mark Bechtel

At first glance it looked like the 1996 season was a bump in the road for Jeff Gordon. Sure, the 1995 champ failed to defend his crown. But he still became the first driver in three years to win 10 times. Such is life under NASCAR's arcane points system, which allowed Gordon's teammate, Terry Labonte, who won just twice but finished second seven times, to win the championship. Dale Earnhardt looked like he was going to be a factor, winning twice by early March, but he failed to take another checkered flag and finished a distant fourth in the points race.

The highlight—if you can call it that—of Earnhardt's season was a spectacular wreck at Talladega in July. While leading the DieHard 500 he was tapped from behind and spun head-on into the wall. He then flipped over and slid on his roof before three cars rammed into him. He was eventually freed from the wreckage, and when he made a point of walking to the ambulance instead of being stretchered, most assumed he was showing his toughness. "Actually, I was dying to lie down on that stretcher," Earnhardt said later. "But it hurt so much just standing that I was afraid if I tried to lie down, I'd faint."

Earnhardt returned—he almost won at Watkins Glen two weeks later—even with a broken sternum and collarbone, but could do no better than a second-place finish the rest of the year. Gordon, for his part, finished the year on a tear, winning three straight races and four of five at one point. But he had suffered six finishes outside of the top 30 (Labonte had just one), and

Earnhardt enjoyed a moment alone (above) before the 1997 California 500. Although Earnhardt's outlaw image had often cast him as the "bad guy," his popularity soared among longtime NASCAR fans who resented Gordon's corporate backing and associated Earnhardt with the good ol' boys of the past.

those bad days cost him a second title.

Still, by the time the '97 season rolled around, about the only thing the 25-year-old hadn't done in his short career was win the Daytona 500. Earnhardt knew a thing or two about that, having been shut out in the sport's biggest race in his first 18 attempts. "I had begun to feel that I was going to fall right in line with Dale and keep on coming close but not winning it," said Gordon. It seemed like something had to give—and after a wild ride, it did.

Late in '96 Gordon's car owner, Rick Hendrick, had been diagnosed with leukemia. His troubles were compounded in December by an indictment related to

his car dealership business. To get his boss's mind off his problems Gordon promised Hendrick, who was watching from home in North Carolina, that he'd have everyone in his house high-fiving by the end of the Daytona 500. Just past the halfway point of the race it looked like Gordon was going to let Hendrick down. His right rear tire had a small cut and a slow leak. Forced to pit, he fell from third place to 31st. But he scrambled back, and with 11 laps left he ran down Earnhardt, who was in second place behind Bill Elliott. As the pair exited Turn 2, Earnhardt got a little loose when Gordon dove to the inside. Earnhardt tapped the

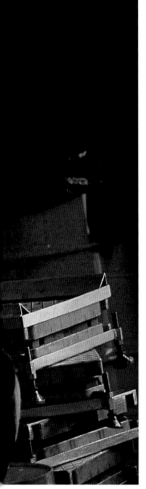

wall, then Gordon. Earnhardt's car then got caught up with Ricky Rudd and Dale Jarrett and ended up doing a somersault. Gordon escaped the danger and was able to run down Elliott with the help of his teammates, Terry Labonte and Ricky Craven. Earnhardt, meanwhile, walked out of the ambulance he had been placed in, got back in his car and finished the race, crossing the line in 31st place. Afterward, he refused to criticize Gordon, saying only that the kid "got maybe a little impatient."

Gordon used the race as a springboard, but Earnhardt never recovered. He was still winless and looking to break a 50-race losing streak in September when the

Southern 500 was run in Darlington. But his behavior on the track that weekend would only intensify the questions about his recent string of poor performances. Gordon was attempting to win the race for the third time in a row, which had never been done. (Earnhardt had won it in '89 and '90, but came up short in '91.) As the field entered Turn 1, Earnhardt inexplicably smacked the wall. He did the same thing in Turn 2 then made two laps around the track in search of the pit entrance. He had blacked out, and sixteen doctors would probe him in the coming days in an effort to find out why. "They didn't check to see if I was pregnant," Earnhardt said, but that

Everyone loves a winner—until he wins too much, that is. Gordon (above, celebrating his 1997 Daytona 500 victory) won 33 races between 1996 and 1998 but endured boos at almost every NASCAR stop.

was just about the only test they omitted.

They never found an answer and Earnhardt never missed a race. One possibility was a lingering injury from the Talladega wreck, an incident that also marked the beginning of the steady decline in his results. "It seems that things are not as great as they were before the Talladega crash," he said. "I don't understand why we haven't won races this year."

Darrell Waltrip, who had suffered a brutal crash at Daytona in 1990, had a clue. "Earnhardt got hurt and he's never been the same," he said. "With old drivers, injuries last longer, and the memories of those injuries last a whole lot longer."

As for the Southern 500, Gordon got the lead and didn't back down from Jeff Burton, who acknowledged he was trying to "knock the s--- out of" Gordon on the last lap. His win brought him a million-dollar bonus from Winston. The victory was Gordon's ninth of the season, and by adding number 10 two weeks later he became the first driver to hit double figures in consecutive years since Waltrip turned the trick in 1981 and '82. Earnhardt, meanwhile, went winless for the first time since 1981.

By the 1998 Daytona 500 the Intimidator's losing streak stood at 59. That, coupled with his 0-for-19 record in NASCAR's marquee event, didn't exactly inspire confidence in his fans. But when Earnhardt took an early lead in the race it looked like the old Dale was back. Gordon, the defending champ, started a poor 29th but zipped through the pack at a lightning pace. By beating Earnhardt out of the

pits on Lap 59, he moved into the lead. About 60 laps later, though, he hit a piece of debris, which damaged his front air dam and took his handling away. The debris was so small that Gordon didn't even know he had hit it. All he knew was that his hopes for another win were gone. Earnhardt passed him on Lap 123 and held on for his greatest victory, while Gordon finished 16th after having late engine problems. "[Earnhardt] did what he does here every year, except he kept doing it all the way to the end," a gracious Gordon said after the race. "We all would have loved to have been in Victory Lane, but we're all real happy for Dale. If we couldn't be there, we all loved for him to be. He's earned it, man. He deserves it."

Most of the NASCAR community echoed Gordon's sentiments. Crewmen from nearly every team mobbed Earnhardt's car as he drove to Victory Lane—after making a detour to cut a large number 3 into the infield grass. "I'm here

Earnhardt (left, with wife, Teresa, and daughter, Taylor) never caught Gordon in the Winston Cup standings in 1998, but he won his first Daytona 500. Gordon (above) claimed his second million-dollar bonus of the year when he won the '98 Southern 500.

and I've got that goddam monkey off my back," he said in Victory Lane, as he produced a small toy monkey and flung it in the direction of the crowd of reporters hanging on his every word. His purse of $1,059,105 was a motorsports record, leaving Earnhardt to wonder jokingly, "What's the $5 for?" Overjoyed, he tried to place the win in perspective. "This is it," he said. "There ain't nothing gonna top this. Well, maybe that eighth championship."

It was big talk, but at the time it seemed reasonable. Gordon went on a tear that summer, however, at one point winning four races in a row and five of six. Earnhardt, meanwhile, went nowhere. Things were so bad after 13 races—just one of which produced a top 5 finish—that owner Richard Childress took Earnhardt's crew chief, Larry McReynolds, and put him with his other driver, Mike Skinner.

Earnhardt's new chief was Kevin Hamlin, who could guide Earnhardt to nothing better than a third-place finish in 19 starts. After departing, McReynolds said that Earnhardt didn't spend enough time at the shop any more and that his distance from his crew was hurting him on the track. "A driver has to be part of a team today," McReynolds said. "Talentwise, Dale's still there, but the competition has certainly caught up, and I question his total focus."

No one was questioning Gordon's focus. In fact the only question people were asking was, Can anyone stop him? Gordon won 13 times in 1998, equalling Richard Petty's modern-era record for victories, and claimed his third Winston Cup title. The only thing, it seemed, that could knock him from his lofty perch was an unforeseen shakeup in his team. And what were the odds of that happening?

Eight Is Great

Dale Earnhardt broke Cale Yarborough's alltime track record with his eighth victory at the Atlanta Motor Speedway.

Leader of the Pack

"I like Atlanta Motor Speedway," said Earnhardt, who started 18th. "I hope Cale is not mad at me for breaking his record."

Making History

Earnhardt may live in North Carolina, but he has made Atlanta his second home. Already the holder of the track speed record (163.633 mph), Earnhardt also set a new record for the Purolator 500 with the winning speed of 161.298 mph.

3.10.96—With 37 laps left in the Purolator 500, Dale Earnhardt entered pit road trailing leader Terry Labonte by one second. But his crew put him back on the track two seconds ahead of Labonte, and Earnhardt ran away with the 70th win of his Winston Cup career and his eighth career victory at Atlanta Motor Speedway. "We had a great pit stop there at the end," Earnhardt said. "I knew when I came down the front straightaway and Terry was just rolling out of pit road that we had a great stop. All I had to do was run the car hard."

Earnhardt refused to let Labonte sneak back into the race, finishing more than four seconds ahead of him. "We've got a great team and I think we're working better today than ever before," Earnhardt said. "Who knows? This could be the year we win [that eighth title]."

Jeff Gordon, who won a week earlier in Richmond, led for 24 laps and finished third.

Earnhardt Rules

Earnhardt and Gordon overcame poor starting positions (18th and 21st, respectively) to lead for 160 combined laps in Atlanta. But it was Earnhardt's day, and he moved up from fourth to second in the Winston Cup standings.

CHANGING OF THE GUARD

75

Taylor Made

Earnhardt and daughter Taylor basked in the glow of his record-breaking eighth Atlanta victory. "That's a proud mark," he said. "I broke the record on the same track that the old guys ran. It means a lot."

Battered but Not Broken

One week after a frightening wreck at Talladega, Dale Earnhardt got back behind the wheel for the Brickyard 400

8.4.96—"I know Dale Earnhardt," Jeff Gordon said. "If he's got a good car and things are going well, there's no way you can drag him out of that race car."

Alas, heading into the 1996 Brickyard 400, things were not going well for Earnhardt. One week earlier, at the DieHard 500 in Talladega, he had broken a collarbone and cracked his sternum in an 11-car wreck. Defending his Brickyard 400 title didn't seem possible. But since drivers earn Winston Cup points as long

as they start the race, Earnhardt steered his car around Indy for the first six laps. At the first caution flag he gave way to relief driver Mike Skinner, who guided number 3 to a 15th-place finish. "It hurt more in my heart than in my body to get out of that car," Earnhardt said. "I didn't want to."

Gordon, the pole sitter and Winston Cup leader, had an equally miserable afternoon. He crashed in Lap 23, finished 37th and dropped to fourth in the standings.

No Pain, No Gain

"I'm still sore in a lot of places I haven't been sore for a while," Earnhardt said. His emotions overwhelmed him when he gave way to Mike Skinner, but the strategy worked as Earnhardt moved up to second in the standings.

Not-so-Happy Birthday

Although Gordon and car owner Rick Hendrick celebrated winning the pole for the Brickyard 400, a blown right-front tire spoiled Gordon's 25th birthday by sending him into the wall on Turn 4.

Feast or Famine

Gordon's crew did what it could to get number 24 back on the track after the accident. Gordon, who entered the race leading the Winston Cup Series in points and wins (6), was able to log 17 more laps in his damaged car before retiring.

"I don't want to take a chance and do something to injure myself or endanger somebody else's life. There's a lot of guys out there with me that I've got to think about."

—*Dale Earnhardt*

Super Sub

Mike Skinner turned in a superb performance after taking over for Earnhardt. "I wasn't that nervous before the race," he said. "The nervousness that I had was for wrecking Dale's car. I did not want to wreck Dale's car."

Gordon Plays Spoiler

Jeff Gordon won his second straight Southern 500 and denied Dale Jarrett the Winston Million

9.1.96—In March 1996 Jeff Gordon's chances of winning a second straight Winston Cup championship looked dead. He was last in the standings after he finished 42nd and 40th in the season's first two major races. "We're coming off a championship season," Gordon said at the time. "You might think things are going to go a certain way, but I think that tough start might have been a blessing in disguise."

Gordon's prophecy proved correct. With his second straight win at the Southern 500, Gordon climbed into second place in the standings, 24 points behind Terry Labonte. The victory—his seventh of the season—prevented Dale Jarrett from collecting Winston's million-dollar bonus for winning three of NASCAR's top four races.

Dale Earnhardt finished 12th after wrecking on Lap 195 but accumulated enough points to remain in fourth place.

Stalking the Leader

Gordon climbed to second place in the Winston Cup standings with his Southern 500 win. "There's a lot of things I haven't done in this sport," he said. "And one is come from behind to chase 'em down."

On a Mission

"It hasn't been a picture-perfect year," said Gordon (above, with Ray Evernham). "Last year, things really went well. This year, we've gone through some down times and

Party Crasher

Although many of the 80,000 fans at Darlington had turned out to see local favorite Dale Jarrett make history, Gordon cooled their enthusiasm and won some new fans with another commanding performance. "I know what a great place this is and how tough it is to win here," said Gordon (with wife Brooke after the victory).

"Dale Jarrett drove his heart out. I hated to see him have those problems. It would have been neat for him to do [the Winston Million], but at the same time, we race to win."

—Jeff Gordon

Second Best

"I wanted to win this race," said Earnhardt (opposite and below), who had struggled in his last 11 races. "I punished the heck out of the tires trying to run Gordon down."

Last Call

Jeff Gordon and Dale Earnhardt finished one-two as NASCAR bid adieu to North Wilkesboro

9.29.96—Since NASCAR's first season in 1949, North Wilkesboro had been a staple of the circuit. Hiding in the shadows of the Appalachian foothills in northwest North Carolina, the historic, .625-mile oval had tested every driver from Johnson to Petty to Yarborough. NASCAR's recent explosion in popularity, however, placed an emphasis on giant superspeedways, making the smaller, more intimate tracks expendable.

Appropriately, it was Jeff Gordon, NASCAR's hottest young driver, who had the last word at Wilkesboro in the Tyson Holly Farms 400. His victory—his third straight and 10th of the season—and the track's farewell combined for a rare combination of NASCAR's past and future. "It's ironic, really," Gordon said. "You look at this racetrack and see where we've been, and the fact that we're not coming back any more is another sign of how far we've come."

The Last Checkered Flag

"It's unfortunate this is going to be the last time we're coming here," Gordon said. "I get more and more comfortable each time here. . . . I really hate to see a place like this go."

1996 Final Winston Cup Standings

	DRIVER	POINTS	EARNINGS ($)
1.	Terry Labonte (2)	4,657	4,030,648
2.	Jeff Gordon (10)	4,620	3,428,485
3.	Dale Jarrett (4)	4,568	2,985,418
4.	Dale Earnhardt (2)	4,327	2,285,926
5.	Mark Martin (0)	4,278	1,887,396

Note: Victories in parentheses.

Fond Farewell

"I know a lot of guys were wanting to win today," Gordon said. "You could see the drive in a lot of guys, especially Dale. That makes [the win] even more special."

Road Warrior

Quieting critics who claimed he couldn't win on a road course, Jeff Gordon won at the Glen

8.10.97—It may not have been Daytona or Talladega or Indy, but Jeff Gordon could not have been any prouder of his Bud at the Glen victory at Watkins Glen. "I think this is one of the most satisfying wins I've ever had," Gordon said. "For me personally, this has been a very difficult transition to race on a road course."

Ever since Gordon burst onto the NASCAR scene, his detractors had slighted his driving skills and attributed much of his success to a superior car. Gordon's victory on the Glen's demanding, winding road course proved them all wrong. "This was a legitimate goal of ours," Gordon said. "We came out this year to win on a road course."

The victory—his eighth of the season—extended his lead in the Winston Cup standings to 109 points over Mark Martin.

Practice Makes Perfect

Gordon led for 32 of the 90 laps. "Every time we go to Watkins Glen or Sears Point, we make notes to try to better ourselves," he said.

Snakebitten

"We can't catch a break," Earnhardt said of his drought. "Nothing but bad luck seems to follow us these days."

"The key to road-course racing is you've got to like it, and I really enjoy it."

—Jeff Gordon

Forty-Seven and Counting

Earnhardt, who ran as high as third during the race, was penalized with a stop-and-go penalty after he ran over an air hose. He finished 16th, extending his career-high winless string to 47 races.

This Bud's for You

Approximately 150,000 fans turned out at Watkins Glen to see Gordon (24) win his first road-course race. He crossed the finish line of the Bud at the Glen 10 car-lengths ahead of Geoff Bodine.

Feeling like a Million

Jeff Gordon became only the second driver in history to claim the Winston Million

8.31.97—It wasn't easy, but Jeff Gordon won his third consecutive Southern 500 and claimed the $1 million Winston bonus for winning three of NASCAR's most prestigious races. During the final laps of the race, Gordon traded bumps with Jeff Burton but held on for the victory in front of 70,000 jubilant fans.

With the victory, Gordon became the first driver to win three consecutive Southern 500's and the only man besides Bill Elliott (1985) to

win the Winston Million. "I earned this one," Gordon said. "For the final 30 laps I got everything out of it I possibly could."

If the end of the race was thrilling, the beginning was baffling. Dale Earnhardt, starting 36th, banged the wall twice on the opening lap and struggled just to get his car back onto pit road. "I saw two race tracks," explained a groggy Earnhardt, who admitted to falling asleep in the car prior to the race.

Jeff vs. Jeff

Gordon and Burton (99) dueled during the final laps. "I saw Jeff coming and I blocked him," Gordon said. "He hit me in the right bumper and I was just glad that I didn't spin."

Asleep at the Wheel

"His voice was very unclear," said Don Hawks, president of Dale Earnhardt, Inc., of his driver during the first few pace laps. "It was not the Dale Earnhardt I knew. . . . We knew right away there was something wrong."

"It really is exciting to me to do things as a team that nobody has done before. When you look at the list of those who have raced here, to know that we've accomplished [three straight wins] is something else."

—Jeff Gordon

Thanks a Million

"This has just been an incredible, unbelievable day," Gordon (with wife, Brooke) said. "I should have never won that race. I didn't think I was going to, but this team never gave up."

1997 ATLANTA

Simply the Best

One day after wrecking his car in practice, Jeff Gordon won his second championship

11.16.97—Someday, Jeff Gordon will learn how to make things easy on himself. In 1995 he won his first Winston Cup championship, but only after he squandered a 205-point lead and held on to win by a scant 34. In addition to another late-season fade in 1997, he nearly ruined everything by slamming into Bobby Hamilton's car in the pit area during Saturday's practice for the season-ending NAPA 500.

On Sunday, starting 37th in a backup car, Gordon steered his way safely to a 17th-place finish to edge Dale Jarrett by 14 points and Mark Martin by 29 in the closest three-way points race in NASCAR history. The victory capped a sensational year for Gordon as he won the Daytona 500, earned the Winston Million and became the first driver to win more than $5 million in a season. "If this isn't written in the dictionary next to 'career year,'" Gordon said. "Then I don't know what is."

O-fer 1997

Earnhardt (opposite) led in the early stages of the NAPA 500 but finished 16th. He concluded the season without a victory for the first time since 1981. Gordon (below), who needed to finish 18th to clinch, narrowly won the title.

"I judge people by talent and ability in different areas, and I think that Jeff Gordon is at the same level of ability as Richard Petty and Dale Earnhardt and Mario Andretti; and he's got a long career ahead of him."

—Ray Evernham

1997 Final Winston Cup Standings

	DRIVER	POINTS	EARNINGS ($)
1.	Jeff Gordon (10)	4,710	6,375,658
2.	Dale Jarrett (7)	4,696	3,240,542
3.	Mark Martin (4)	4,681	2,532,484
4.	Jeff Burton (3)	4,285	2,296,614
5.	Dale Earnhardt (0)	4,216	2,151,909

Note: Victories in parentheses.

Twice as Nice

Gordon's second championship didn't come easy. "We appreciate this one more than the first, especially after not winning it last year," Gordon said.

One for the Ages

"I never believed, when guys told me how it felt to win the 500," Earnhardt said. "I never believed, but I do now. It sure feels good."

All Hail King Dale!

After 19 years of misfortune, Dale Earnhardt finally won the Daytona 500

2.15.98—As Dale Earnhardt celebrated in Victory Lane, one could not help but think of the words of Mark Twain: "Rumors of my death have been greatly exaggerated."

Earnhardt had not won a race in nearly two years—a streak that spanned 59 races—and at age 46 his career was mostly in the rearview mirror. When you consider Earnhardt's freakish bad luck in his sport's biggest race, his chances to finally win the Daytona 500 appeared slim. But he qualified fourth and was among the leaders all afternoon. He refused to give up the lead after Lap 140, and when a yellow flag appeared following a tangle on the backstretch during the final lap, Earnhardt and 185,000 racing fans knew the elusive title was finally his. "We cried a little on that lap coming in to get that checkered flag," he said. "It was pretty awesome. All the race teams were giving me high fives."

Team Effort

Earnhardt's crew was poetry in motion during the Daytona
500. But even as they celebrated his first 500 victory, their
eyes were set on another goal: winning a record-breaking
eighth Winston Cup championship.

500-Pound Gorilla

"There," Earnhardt said with a smile. "That monkey's off my back." Never again would he have to answer the dreaded question, "Will you ever win the Daytona 500?"

Worth the Wait

After kissing the hood of his car, Earnhardt celebrated with his family and friends. "You won't have to wake me [tomorrow]," he said. "I ain't going to bed."

"He got the lead when he needed to, and from then on he controlled the race. We all want to win the Daytona 500, but as many times as he's been so close, so close, he deserves it."

—Jeff Gordon

Texas NASCAR Massacre

Mark Martin won a crash-filled Texas 500 as drivers complained about track conditions

4.5.98—By the time Mark Martin had taken the checkered flag at the Texas 500, he didn't want to hear any more about the track. "I am sick and tired of racetrack bashing," Martin said. "It's a great opportunity for the race fans. It was a great show."

A great show? Maybe. But after a second-lap pileup relegated two of the sport's biggest drawing cards to the status of also-rans, the race lost some of its luster. "It just isn't excit-ing with [Earnhardt] and Gordon out," said one race fan. The Chevrolets belonging to Jeff Gordon and Dale Earnhardt were just two of the 10 cars that were damaged in the Turn 1 fiasco, adding to complaints that the course was unraceable. Drivers complained that there was water seeping through the pavement and that there wasn't enough room to pass.

After extensive repairs, both drivers made it back on the track but never threatened to win.

All Hands on Deck

Even Earnhardt got his hands dirty as his crew frantically worked to fix his car's tail section after the accident. Although his car missed 129 laps, the crew completed the repairs, and Earnhardt finished 35th.

Rough Ride

Gordon (above) had to replace half of his car's front end, but like Earnhardt, he finished the race, placing 31st.

"They had a massacre down here some-where, but I forget what it was called. Oh yeah, the Alamo. That's what this was."

—Darrell Waltrip

Gordon Breaks Bank

Jeff Gordon won his second Brickyard 400 and took home a record $1.6 million

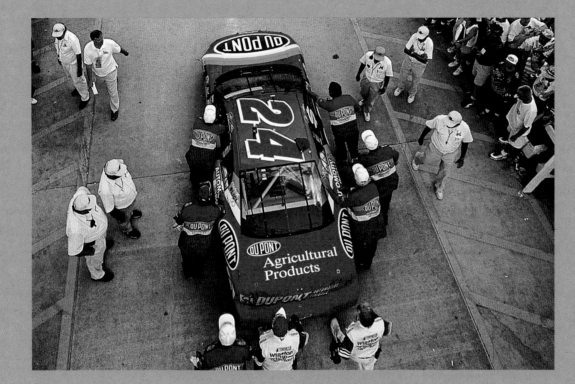

8.1.98—For the second time in the five-year history of the Brickyard 400, local favorite Jeff Gordon took a victory lap. This time, though, he had company. An armored truck, representing the $1 million bonus he earned from Winston, followed him around, and when all the dough was counted, Gordon would take home more than $1.6 million—the largest payout for a single race in American sports history.

Gordon, who finished under caution after a wreck on the second-to-last lap, took the advantage when Dale Jarrett ran out of gas. "We were flat lucky today," said Ray Evernham. "We didn't win the race. There were a couple of faster Fords that lost it."

Gordon, who had won the Coca-Cola 600 in May, became the first driver to claim the new Winston Million. The bonus rewards drivers who win a major race if they had finished in the top 5 in the previous major race.

Who Wants to Be a Millionaire

"I was in the hunt all day," said Dale Earnhardt, who finished fifth and qualified for the Winston bonus at the next major race, the Southern 500. The Rainbow Warriors (opposite) helped Gordon find Victory Lane.

Follow the Rainbow

Gordon, ahead as he passed the scoring pylon, led for more than half the race. "I know we brought some serious horsepower this week," Gordon said. "It was the most we've ever had."

Million-Dollar Smile

"To win this race twice, and the million dollars, and to do it with Mark Martin on my tail was just amazing," Gordon said. "I don't know if I can take it all in right now. This just blows me away."

No Place like Home

In stark contrast to the hostile greetings he often received elsewhere, the Indy crowd supported Gordon all weekend. "The Indianapolis Motor Speedway just holds so much prestige in itself, but then you come here and you've got people pulling for you," Gordon said after the race. "It is important to get cheers."

"We have the Michael Jordan of NASCAR racing driving our car."

—*Ray Evernham*

Gordon Clinches No. 3

Jeff Gordon won his third title with a record-breaking victory at the AC Delco 400

11.1.98—Jeff Gordon had already clinched his third Winston Cup championship by leading Lap 120 of the AC Delco 400, but in his mind he still hadn't "won" it. "We want to come out winning and not only win the championship, but win races when we win the championship," Gordon said.

Gordon accomplished just that, winning in record time for his 12th victory of the season and his third championship in the last four years. He joined Lee and Richard Petty, Dale Earnhardt, David Pearson, Darrell Waltrip and Cale Yarborough as the only men to win three titles, and at 27, he was by far the youngest.

Gordon suffered a 15-second pit penalty on Lap 267 and led for only 28 laps, but he caught Rusty Wallace with eight laps to go and held off Dale Jarrett at the end for the win. "It's a big relief," Gordon said. "I don't have to worry about going to Atlanta [for the season-ending race]."

A Racer's Dozen

Gordon's Rockingham victory was his 12th of the season—the most by a driver since Darrell Waltrip in 1982. "It has been one of those incredible years," Gordon said. "It seems like we couldn't do anything wrong."

Making His Mark

Gordon celebrated his championship by spinning a few donuts through the NASCAR 50th anniversary emblem in front of Rockingham's main grandstand.

1998 Final Winston Cup Standings

	DRIVER	POINTS	EARNINGS ($)
1.	Jeff Gordon (13*)	5,328	6,175,867
2.	Mark Martin (7)	4,964	3,279,370
3.	Dale Jarrett (3)	4,619	3,368,735
4.	Rusty Wallace (1)	4,501	2,133,435
5.	Jeff Burton (2)	4,415	2,114,597
8.	Dale Earnhardt (1)	3,928	2,611,100

Note: Victories in parentheses.   *Won NAPA 500 on 11/8 for 13th victory

Under Caution

1999–2000

Gordon (opposite, 24) led Earnhardt in the 2000 NAPA AutoCare 500 at Martinsville, but the Intimidator later passed him and finished second, behind Tony Stewart. Earnhardt and Gordon chatted around Gordon's car (left) before the 2000 Winston—a highlight of Earnhardt's season, not only because of his own third-place finish, but because his son Dale Jr. won it.

Under Caution

by Mark Bechtel

"We've got no friends out here."

That's what Jeff Gordon radioed to his crew chief, Ray Evernham, during the 1999 Daytona 500.

"Yeah," came the answer, "but you knew that."

"I felt about the loneliest out there today that I've ever felt," Gordon said later. "There were times when [cars] were right behind me, and I thought, Oh, yeah, they're going to give me that aerodynamic push right on by whoever I was trying to pass. Then—pheeooo!—they'd just go away. They'd push me enough to help me get side-by-side with a car, and then they'd make sure I was left out there by myself. But you know what? I don't expect any different. [The loneliness felt] almost like an honor."

Gordon earned that honor in 1998, arguably the finest season by a driver in NASCAR's modern era, when he won 13 of 33 races and took home $9.3 million with bonuses. The extent to which the Winston Cup circuit had taken on an everyone-against-Gordon flavor was never more evident than at Daytona, where winning without help is all but impossible. But even after being left hung out to dry all day, he was still hanging around the front of the pack at the finish. With ten laps left, he dove onto the apron in Turn 1 to get underneath leader Rusty Wallace. He almost ran into the back of the lapped car of Ricky Rudd, but just before making contact, he veered in front of Wallace and took the lead. Wallace was miffed after the race, calling the daring move foolish. "It could

have taken a lot of people out—and killed some people too," Wallace said. "It's something that can lose you a lot of respect from your competitors."

There was some irony in that statement. If anything had caused Gordon to lose the respect of his colleagues, it was his squeaky clean image and his propensity to show his emotions as he did when he won his first race in Charlotte in 1994—Wallace and Earnhardt had been quick to razz him then. Even more ironic was the fact that Gordon's final move at Daytona was made possible by some help from Earnhardt. With 25 laps left, both drivers pitted under caution, which dropped them back in the pack. Their crews consulted, and Evernham told Gordon, "Dale wants to work with you."

"I'll help him all the way up to second place," Gordon answered. "I'd love to work with him."

When the green flag fell, however, Earnhardt took off. After 10 laps Gordon

Evernham (above right, during the 1999 MBNA Gold 400 at Dover Downs—his final race with Hendrick Motorsports) left Gordon to create his own success with Dodge. Earnhardt had an excellent 2000 season as a driver and owner. His son Dale Jr. (opposite, right) won two races for the old man.

finally caught him, and they began to work as a most unlikely alliance. Earnhardt was up to second and Gordon was third, and it looked like they were going to track down Wallace together. But with 12 laps left, Gordon suddenly pulled out from behind Earnhardt and got a push from Mike Skinner—Earnhardt's teammate—past the Intimidator and into position to pass Wallace. Earnhardt stayed close but could never get any help in the final laps. "I got beat," Earnhardt said simply after the race. He congratulated Gordon, but he did it in typical Intimidator fashion—with a bump. "He drove into the side of me," Gordon said, "and just waved."

The next week at Rockingham something happened that was even more bizarre than

a Gordon-Earnhardt alliance. Gordon's
engine blew. In 1997 and '98, Gordon finished 61 of the 65 races he started, which
was as much a testament to his crew chief,
Evernham, as it was to his driving skills.
But in '99 car problems were far more fre-
quent. Gordon would ultimately win a cir-
cuit-best seven races, but seven DNFs
kept him out of the points race, which was
won by Dale Jarrett. He finished sixth, one
spot ahead of Earnhardt.

But had Gordon won another Winston
Cup title, what would that have proved?
Evernham, for one, was troubled by that
question. To a certain extent Evernham's
reputation would always hinge on
Gordon's. He wanted a bigger role, and
with car owner Rick Hendrick fighting
leukemia, he had all but taken over the
day-to-day operation of Hendrick
Motorsports. A deal to make Evernham
the chief operating officer of the business
was arranged, but late in the summer
Evernham decided to take a job overseeing
Dodge's return to Winston Cup racing. It
was a chance to build something from
scratch—and a chance to accomplish
something without Gordon. "You're 42

As the drivers
with bull's-eyes
on their backs,
Gordon and
Earnhardt did not
hesitate to team
up—as they did
in the 1999
Daytona 500
(above)—if it
served both their
purposes.

years old and you've been presented with the greatest opportunity you're going to have in racing to prove that you can do something," said Evernham. "I just kept thinking about where I was headed, what I had accomplished, and when I'm gone from this earth what I'd like to be remembered for. If I could do this and be successful at it, then I'd prove I am a good racer."

Evernham left following the fall race in Dover, Del., and Gordon quickly answered those who questioned how he'd do without his old guru by winning consecutive races at Martinsville and Charlotte. Following the season, Hendrick hired Robbie Loomis away from Petty Racing to be Gordon's new chief. "I knew with Jeff and Ray that there wasn't any magic or anything," Loomis said. "It was just a case of them communicating well and Ray's being able to get inside Jeff's head."

But there were other changes in the works. The Rainbow Warriors, Gordon's mercenary pit crew, were hired away by Jarrett. With a new crew chief and new crew, Gordon won three races in 2000 and had his worst points finish since his rookie season. That doesn't mean the future is bleak. Gordon only needs to look at his old rival to see that developing chemistry between a driver and a crew chief takes

Six years and several crew changes separated Earnhardt's first and second Winston Cup titles. After unparalleled success early in his career, only time will tell how long Gordon (right, celebrating his 1999 Daytona win) will need to adjust to his new team.

time. While Gordon was struggling in 2000, Earnhardt and his crew chief, Kevin Hamlin, who came on board midway through the 1998 season, finally began to mesh. Earnhardt said the more he worked with Hamlin, the more he was reminded of Kirk Shelmerdine, who guided his crew for so many years. In order to pair Hamlin and Earnhardt, owner Richard Childress broke up the much-touted—but largely unsuccessful—team of Earnhardt and Larry McReynolds. "Man, I'm so happy Richard made that change," said Earnhardt. "I haven't regretted it one bit, and I love Larry to death. But Kevin is more my style of crew chief. The guy is constantly thinking, he never quits on making the car better, and he's not the kind of guy who blows up and kicks and screams. He's the kind of guy who will sit down and listen to what I say."

Other drivers noticed a change in Earnhardt, who had become more and more busy running Dale Earnhardt, Inc. (DEI), but seemed to rededicate himself to racing in 2000. "I see Dale Earnhardt driving harder and more aggressive than I've seen him the last three years," said Jeff Burton. His son, and top DEI driver, agreed. "He's been a lot more excited about each race," said Dale Earnhardt Jr., who gave his old man something to be proud of when he won twice as a rookie in 2000.

The year 2001 will see a few milestones. Earnhardt turns 50 in April; yet he shows no signs of letting up in his quest for that elusive eighth Winston Cup championship. Gordon won't be 30 until later that season; he has plenty of time to add to his three championships. Their dominance in the last decade, however, has been challenged by other racing teams who have worked hard to narrow the gap. NASCAR today is as competitive as ever. Fourteen different drivers won races during the 2000 season, the most since 1991. Jarrett, Stewart, the Labontes and the Burtons are here to stay. But there are still two cars that fans look for first and that other drivers dread to see on their bumpers: NASCAR's best rivalry is as strong as ever.

High Noon

Jeff Gordon outdueled Dale Earnhardt in an electrifying Daytona 500 showdown

2.14.99—The rivalry between Jeff Gordon and Dale Earnhardt reached a fever pitch as the two drivers went *mano a mano* for the final laps of the Daytona 500. Gordon, who slipped past Rusty Wallace with 10 laps left, held off a relentless Intimidator to win his second Daytona title.

Gordon, coming off a season in which he tied Richard Petty's record of 13 victories, quickly learned he was on his own at Daytona.

"Every time I tried to make a move," Gordon said, "they made sure they hung me out to dry." But he narrowly maneuvered between Wallace and Ricky Rudd to take the lead. Earnhardt followed him and did everything he could to get by. "I knew if he got in front of me, there was no way I was going to get back by him," Gordon said. Gordon held on—barely— and Earnhardt communicated his respect with a gentle bump during Gordon's victory lap.

Close Quarters

Gordon and Earnhardt went head-to-head in a dash to the finish. "He was definitely bumping me back there and I wanted him to," Gordon said. "I was saying, 'Come on, hit me harder.' "

Daytona Duel

"Even though we battled for a championship in '95, we really didn't get to have many tight battles all the way to the finish," Gordon said. "I really can't think of a better way to do it than here at the Daytona 500."

Close Encounter

Gordon breathed a sigh of relief after out-sprinting Earnhardt to the finish line. "I was watching him in the mirrors so much that I had to be careful to watch where I was going," Gordon admitted.

"To me, winning this race is much sweeter and more meaningful because I was battling the guy I learned from. But that was the longest 10 laps of my life."

—*Jeff Gordon*

Ready for Takeoff

Gordon caught some air during his qualifying run (below) but that was only a taste of things to come. In Turn 7 of Lap 51, he drove completely off the track, giving up the lead and falling to third place.

California Dreamin'

After driving clear off the track, a flu-stricken Jeff Gordon won the Save Mart/Kragen 350

6.27.99—Jeff Gordon fought off the flu and Mark Martin to win the Save Mart/Kragen 350 at Sears Point Raceway in Sonoma, Calif. It was his fourth straight road course victory—a Winston Cup record—and his fourth win of the season.

Although he started from the pole and led for 80 of the race's 112 laps, Gordon's day was anything but easy. His seat belt became undone, he bungled some gear shifts and on Lap 51 he drove clear off the track. At one point,

the team considered changing drivers, but Gordon wouldn't allow it. "For a while I didn't think we were going to finish the race, let alone win it," Gordon said. "I felt myself starting to deteriorate. I started making mistakes."

A yellow flag on Lap 78 helped Gordon recover, and a red flag came out on Lap 108 that set up a three-lap sprint for the finish between Gordon and Martin. Martin hugged Gordon's bumper but couldn't get by.

Tough Break

Earnhardt, who started 23rd, finished a respectable ninth but could have finished higher if not for some bad luck. On Lap 30 he spun after being bumped by Kenny Schrader.

California Whine Country

"If I wasn't on the radio, I'd say something terrible about the race track," Earnhardt told his crew during the race.

"My biggest concern isn't winning the championship or not dropping out of races; it's getting that edge back."

—Ray Evernham

Drive for Five

Jeff Gordon claimed his fifth straight road course race by winning the Frontier at the Glen.

8.15.99—"It's not hard for me to go back just three or four years ago when a good race for me was if I stayed on the racetrack and didn't miss a shift," Jeff Gordon said. My, how times have changed. Gordon cruised to victory at the 220.5-mile Frontier at the Glen, his fifth straight road course victory and his third consecutive win at Watkins Glen. Starting third, Gordon led for 55 of the 90 laps, including the final 20.

Dale Earnhardt had a memorable race for several reasons. The race marked his 600th consecutive Winston Cup start—a streak dating back to 1979. Unfortunately for the Intimidator, the race itself would be remembered for an incident that occurred on Lap 16. Earnhardt nudged teammate Mike Skinner and spun him out. "He's [mad] that I passed him," screamed an incensed Skinner, who recovered to finish ninth. Earnhardt's day only got worse when he crashed on the final lap and finished 20th.

On the Road Again

Gordon celebrated his fifth win of the season with a blast of champagne (below). "It's nice to see everything go flawless for us today," said Gordon, who had five DNFs in 1999 through Watkins Glen.

600 and Counting

Earnhardt acknowledged the crowd before the
race. Only Terry Labonte's streak of 623 straight
Winston Cup events exceeded the Intimidator's.

*"We like to win and we like to win champi-
onships, and we know what it feels like to
do that. At the end of the year, if we're not
the champion, we're going to feel like we
didn't accomplish our goals."*

—*Jeff Gordon*

Forgettable

Earnhardt bumped his own teammate on Lap 16 and ended his day in the padding of Turn 11 on Lap 90. "That 600th start was pretty sorry," Earnhardt said. "It isn't one I want to remember."

Outfoxing the Field

Wily Dale Earnhardt started 27th but chased down the leaders to win the Winston 500

10.17.99—Unlike the fabled old soldier who "just fades away," Dale Earnhardt refuses to go quietly into retirement. At Talladega, NASCAR's longest and fastest venue, the Intimidator used all of his experience to win the Winston 500. The come-from-behind victory was his third of the year, equaling the number of races he had won in the previous three seasons combined.

Talladega has always agreed with Earnhardt. He has won there eight other times, including last April's DieHard 500. "Earnhardt's the best there is [at restrictor-plate racing] . . . ," said Jeff Gordon, whose 12th-place finish snapped his two-race winning streak. "I don't know how he does it. I watch him in awe."

Earnhardt's victory and strong 1999 season erased any doubts about his future. "We're going to win that eighth championship; that's the goal," said owner Richard Childress, who planned to sign Earnhardt to another long-term contract.

Black Magic

Earnhardt (below, 3) came from farther back (27th) than any previous Talladega winner. After sweeping Talladega's two 1999 races he embraced his wife, Teresa (opposite).

Smooth Move

On Lap 140, Earnhardt gained a stategic advantage when he decided to take a full pit stop during a caution flag, while other drivers rushed back on the track to beat the pace car.

1999 Final Winston Cup Standings

	DRIVER	POINTS	EARNINGS ($)
1.	Dale Jarrett (4)	5,262	3,608,829
2.	Bobby Labonte (5)	5,061	3,550,341
3.	Mark Martin (2)	4,943	2,783,296
4.	Tony Stewart (3)	4,774	2,615,226
5.	Jeff Burton (6)	4,733	5,211,301
6.	Jeff Gordon (7)	4,620	5,281,361
7.	Dale Earnhardt (3)	4,492	2,712,089

Note: Victories in parentheses.

Talladega Sweep

Earnhardt really cleaned up with his second Talladega win of the season and the ninth of his career. He pocketed $120,290 and climbed to seventh in the Winston Cup standings.

Civil War

Dale Jarrett won his third Daytona 500 with the help of Jeff Gordon's old pit crew

2.20.00—With a new pit crew that included five ex-Rainbow Warriors, Dale Jarrett cruised to the third Daytona 500 victory of his career. "The Fantastics," Jarrett suggested as a nickname for his new crew. Jeff Gordon, still reeling from Ray Evernham's departure, may have missed his old crew's services, but even they couldn't have prevented his misfortune: An oil leak on Lap 32 dropped him from contention and he finished 34th.

In an intriguing subplot, the Earnhardts sparked their first family feud. Dale Jr., driving in his first 500, finished 13th—eight spots ahead of his father and car owner—but clashed with the Intimidator. "He didn't work at all with nobody," the elder Earnhardt said. *Au contraire, papa.* At one point, Dale Jr. teamed up with Jarrett to pass his dad. "That was pretty cool," Jarrett said with a smile. "[But] he better remember who signs his paycheck."

It's the Pits

Gordon (opposite, with team manager Brian Whitesell, and below, making a pit stop) started 11th, but an oil leak on Lap 32 sent him behind the pit wall and dropped him to 34th place by the time the checkered flag came out.

Outgunned

Even before the oil leak, Gordon had doubts as to whether he could repeat at Daytona: "I couldn't run with those Fords," he said. "I think we would have been able to get up to about fifth or sixth, but that's about it."

Father Knows Best

"I thought my dad would be the first one to help me," Dale Jr. said of his father (above). "But he was the last person who wanted to stay behind me."

"[NASCAR founder] Mr. Bill France Sr. probably rolled over in his grave if he saw that deal."

—Dale Earnhardt, describing the dull racing at Daytona due to new rules and restrictions

Chip Off the Old Block

Dale Jr. (8) certainly learned one thing from his father: Once you're on the track, it's all business. Although they were teammates, the two Earnhardts didn't seem eager to help each other out during the 500.

Back on Track

Seizing the lead with six laps to go, Jeff Gordon held on for his first win in six months

4.16.00—Between February 1995 and October '99, Jeff Gordon was like the New York Yankees of NASCAR: He won so much that fans started rooting against him, loudly. Even he understood it. "Everyone likes a winner," he said, "but nobody likes someone who wins too much. When I first heard the boos, I said, 'I don't blame 'em.'"

But all that changed in 2000 when Gordon and his new crew chief, Robbie Loomis, strug-gled to crack the top 5, much less win. They finished no better than eighth in the first seven races of 2000, giving the Gordon haters new ammunition: The real reason behind his success, they claimed, was departed crew chief Ray Evernham. With six laps remaining in the DieHard 500, Gordon slipped inside of Jeremy Mayfield and Mark Martin to take the lead, then held off Mike Skinner to seize his 50th career victory and silence his critics. For now.

I'll Take the Low Road

With six laps to go, Gordon ducked down and took the inside track to the winner's circle, where he celebrated with Loomis (opposite).

In His Father's Tiretracks

Dale Earnhardt Jr. (8), who would finish 42nd in the DieHard 500, trailed his dad, who placed third, around a turn at the start of the race.

2000 Final Winston Cup Standings

	DRIVER	POINTS	EARNINGS ($)
1.	Bobby Labonte (4)	5,130	4,041,746
2.	Dale Earnhardt (2)	4,865	3,701,391
3.	Jeff Burton (4)	4,836	5,121,354
4.	Dale Jarrett (2)	4,684	5,225,499
5.	Ricky Rudd (0)	4,575	2,385,404
9.	Jeff Gordon (3)	4,361	2,703,586

Note: Victories in parentheses.

Twenty-Four Returns to the Fore

Gordon won for the first time in six months, but it was not easy: He lost the lead five times during the first 159 laps and had to rally from ninth place with 18 laps to go.

The Fans

Poster Boy

Gordon attracted a crowd at Daytona in 1999. The young
driver's good looks have won and lost him fans. It has been
said that Gordon draws so many boos at racetracks because
the men in attendence are trying to drown out the women
who are cheering him.

Are you a Gordon fan or an Earnhardt fan? In
some parts of the country the answer to that
question does not just define you as a NASCAR
fan but as a person as well. The Earnhardt-
Gordon rivalry would not be as strong if it
weren't for the intense loyalties of their fans.
And although some fans might go too far with
their passions, the rivalry has been wonderful
for the sport of stock car racing. Between 1990
and 1999 NASCAR's attendance nearly doubled.
Television ratings skyrocketed and new motor
speedways in Texas, California and Nevada
have hosted sell-out crowds—a sure sign that
NASCAR has shed its regional roots and boot-
legging image.

Gordon and Earnhardt don't win every race.
In fact, they combined for only five victories in
34 races in 2000. But they are still the two drivers that fans most like to cheer for or root
against. The Kid may no longer be a kid, and the
Outlaw may no longer be an outlaw, but they
will always remain so in the eyes of their fans.

Chipper Dale

Perhaps less intimidating without his trademark moustache, Earnhardt obliged a young fan with an autograph at the Brickyard in 1999.

Far Eastern Frenzy

When NASCAR went to Japan for the first time in 1996, racing officials and PR people had to serve as human barriers between high-profile drivers like Earnhardt (below, handing a picture back to an admirer) and his new fans.

Small World

Even in Japan the Earnhardt and Gordon rivalry divided couples and families. NASCAR's exhibition races in Japan proved that the sport was not only growing nationally, but internationally as well.

"We put on a great show, especially at the end with me and Dale racing hard."

—Jeff Gordon, after the 1996 race in Japan

The Next Generation

The contrast between racing fans in the 1970s and those of today was obvious when you saw the young faces that turned out for the 1996 Brickyard 400.

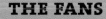

Family Affair

Although fresh faces like Gordon were largely responsible for the influx of new racing fans in the 1990s, some youngsters—like this family in Martinsville in 1997—still preferred the traditional colors of the Intimidator.

"*[Gordon] shouldn't be allowed to be that young, that talented, that experienced and that good looking.*"

—*Dale Jarrett, jokingly explaining why some drivers and fans resent Gordon*

A Van Divided

It must have been a long ride home for at least one of the race fans who went to the 1998 Pepsi Southern 500 at Darlington Raceway in the van below. Gordon won and Earnhardt finished fourth.

Black Flag
Die-hard race fans, like this Earnhardt supporter at the 1998
Pennsylvania 500, are not known for hiding their loyalties.

*"One woman wanted me to drive the hearse for her
husband's funeral."*

*—Dale Earnhardt,
citing an example of the
devotion and loyalty of his fans*

INDEX

Numerals in italics indicate an illustration of the subject mentioned.

PHOTO CREDITS

All photos by George Tiedemann except:

12, 15, DMP Archives; 13-14, International Motor
Sports Hall of Fame; 16-17, Heinz Kluetmeier;
18, John Iacono; 22, Bill Taylor/Daytona Racing
Archives; 23, Classmates.com Yearbook Archives;
25, Daytona Racing Archives.